MW00936119

Praise for Releasing Your Brave Love

The Bible is not merely a book we are to look at; it's the book God gives us to look *through*. Only through the lens of Scripture can we make sense of the world. This is no moralistic, therapeutic devotional. By following closely the storyline of the Scriptures, and clarifying who we are as made in the image of God, Susanne Maynes points students to a faith defined by clarity and engagement.

—***John Stonestreet,*** *President,*
Colson Center for Christian Worldview

I love how Susanne has created a devotional that invites children into God's story for the world and grounds their identity in the image of God. Once their security is established in the gospel, children will be able to see the beauty in all people and will be inspired to reach out to image-bearers whom others might marginalize.

— ***David Eaton,*** *Axis President and Co-founder*

A smart, honest, and inspiring devotional resource for kids. Discusses "put-down, picked-on, and pushed-aside" people with an an appeal to a kid's inner courage and brave heart. Faces head-on the heavy issues forced on today's kids daily. So many excellent insights and eye-opening observations geared to a kid's level. A message ripe for our quickly changing times. May this book be an instrument for stirring alive and raising up many in this upcoming generation to their God-given tasks!

*—**Janet Chester Bly**, author and co-author with award-winning western Stephen Bly, of numerous fiction and non-fiction books for kids and adults, Website: www.BlyBooks.com*

Susanne Maynes has a unique ability to connect with readers of all ages. This devotional helps children develop a deeper understanding of God's love and realize they can be world changers—not someday, but right now.

*— **Kirk Walden**, Pro-life Speaker and Author of The Wall*

Susanne tackles relevant topics that apply to kids' daily lives in language kids can understand. This devotional lays a foundation that children are made in God's image, clearly articulates the gospel, and gives practical examples of how kids can exercise brave love to the world around them. I encourage every parent to read this devotional with their children and pray together for God's truths to come alive. I will purchase this book for all four of my children to read with my grandchildren.

*— **Cindy Latella**, Teacher, MEd in Curriculum and Instruction, Former Children's Church Leader for 20 years*

Releasing Your Brave Love

Helping Kids to Change Their World

By Susanne Maynes

ISBN: 9781731087294

Book jacket: Ken Raney
Interior design: Word-2-Kindle
Cover photography: AdobeStock

Printed in the United States of America

For more information on this author, visit *susannemaynes.com.*

For Reuel, Aviella, Zaccai, Helaina
and my grandchildren yet to come,
all created in *Imago Dei*:

May your brave love change the world for Jesus.

Table of Contents

Foreword: To the Parents of the Reader

What I hope to accomplish in these pages is to help your child gain the following:

- a solid grasp on *Imago Dei* (humans are created in God's image)
- a clear understanding of the gospel, and a healthy sense of self-worth
- an invitation to participate in Christ's kingdom work
- a challenge to stretch beyond their social comfort zone
- a passion for exercising brave love toward all people

This is not necessarily a beginner's devotional. Rather, it's meant to challenge and inspire children who already have a basic understanding of Christianity and want to grow in their faith. I've sprinkled seeds of thought throughout this book which can lead to family discussions on topics like apologetics, evangelism and healthy sexuality. I've also included a list of resources in the back which will help you continue building strong faith in your children.

Kids have great zeal, but they are also vulnerable and may need help with discernment and wisdom. As your son or daughter is inspired to help others, you can help him or her stay safe by being personally involved and providing good instructions and proper boundaries.

Here's the thing: our kids aren't meant to change the world *someday*. Jesus values their input and their influence *right now*. So let's equip them. Let's spend time on the conversations that matter.

Let's make sure they can articulate and live the truth of *Imago Dei* out loud wherever they go.

For this generation,

Susanne

Welcome to an Adventure

Hi, there!

I'm so glad you're reading this book! I bet you are a caring person. I bet that's why you want to read about releasing your brave love. You don't like the unfair and mean things that you see happening in the world, and you'd like to make a difference.

I don't like unfair, mean things, either. If you're anything like me, you'd like to do something about bullies and wrongdoing–but the idea of standing up to that stuff can be scary.

I think you and I have a lot of brave love inside of us, but we need to learn how to release it. I'll explain.

When I was younger, my family owned a beautiful German shepherd dog named Caesar. My father wanted Caesar to help protect the business he owned, so we sent him to watchdog training.

We had to leave our dog with the trainers for a few days. The day we went to pick him up, the trainers told us to watch what Caesar had learned from a place where he couldn't see us.

One man brought Caesar out into the training yard on a leash. Another man put special padding on his arms to protect himself. Then the first man took the leash off Caesar and commanded, "Watch him!"

What happened next shocked us. Our sweet doggie snarled and bared his fangs. He leaped at the man and bit hard into the padding on his arm. Caesar was transformed from our silly, playful puppy to a serious watchdog!

Our dog had to be trained and then let off his leash before

we could see how powerfully able he was to protect us and our property.

This brave love inside you needs to be trained and let loose, too. Then you will see that you can really make a difference when it comes to how the people around you treat each other.

Of course, you're not going to attack people the way a watchdog might attack a robber—it's more like your words and actions will attack the problem of evil.

You might think, *I'm just a kid. What can I do against evil?*

That's what you're going to find out on this adventure!

First, you have to understand God's story and your part in his story. You are very special to God and you were made to reflect his love to other people. We'll talk about how you can have a friendship with him and become part of his family. Once that happens, you'll be able to release the brave love he put in your heart.

You may think you're just a kid—but in the battle against evil, you can make a difference that no one else can.

So, are you ready to begin?

Part 1

Made in God's Image

"Then God said, 'Let us make mankind in our image, in our likeness' … so God created mankind in his own image, in the image of God he created them; male and female he created them."

—Genesis 1:26-28

What Does "Made in God's Image" Mean?

"Then God said, 'Let us make mankind in our image, in our likeness' ... so God created mankind in his own image, in the image of God he created them; male and female he created them." –Genesis 1:26-28

Once upon a time ... there was a giant soup of black, empty nothingness. That's a weird beginning for a story, right? But that's exactly how the very first chapter of the Bible describes the earth before it was formed.

Then God began creating: first light, then sky, water and land. Next, he made trees and plants, and the sun, moon and stars. Then he filled the ocean with swimming creatures and the sky with birds. Last, he made all sorts of land animals—everything from cows to lizards to bugs.

God made all these things by simply commanding them to exist, but then he created one special creature in a different way. He shaped the first human being from the dust of the ground and breathed life into him. Then he created the first woman out of one of the man's ribs (Gen. 2:21-23).

Human beings are the only creatures God made in his own image. What does that mean?

The Old Testament part of the Bible was written in Hebrew. In Hebrew, the word for image is *eikon* (I-con). It means to be like a picture or statue of someone.

When people say something like, "He's the spitting image of his grandfather!" they're talking about a boy who looks or acts a lot like his grandpa. Or if a girl sees her reflection in a mirror, the reflection isn't really her, but it looks like her. It's her image.

That's what it means to be made "in the image of God." Theologians—people who study the Bible deeply—call this *Imago Dei* (I-mah-go Day-ee). (That's how you say "image of God" in another important, old language called Latin.) *Imago Dei* means we reflect God in a way that other creatures don't.

Every boy and girl is a very special creation—including you.

Reflection: Do people ever tell you that you look or act a lot like your mom or dad, or another relative? It can be a pleasant feeling to know you're like a person that you love. It's even better to know that you reflect God somehow, just by being created in his image!

Prayer Point: *God, thank you for creating me in a way that reflects your image. Help me to learn more about what this means so I can understand how very valuable I am.*

Are Pets People, Too?

"God blessed them and said to them, 'Be fruitful and increase in number; fill the earth and subdue it. Rule over the fish in the sea and the birds in the sky and over every living creature that moves on the ground.'"
–Genesis 1:28

When I was a girl, our family had a little dog named Rip who could run so fast he would follow my school bus all the way across town. Later, my kids had a cat named Gizmo who was really smart and loved to ride on our shoulders. I've had other pets, too: dogs, cats, birds, rabbits, gerbils, and even a white rat.

Maybe you have a special pet, too. Pets can be wonderful companions, and caring for them helps us learn to be responsible.

Have you heard the saying, "Animals are people, too?" Do you think that's true? God cares about animals, and he wants us to be kind to them (Prov. 12:10). But animals are not made to reflect God's image as people are.

The Hebrew word *eikon*, which means image, also has to do with something called "dominion." God put humans (who are made in his image) in charge of the animals (who are not). We are supposed to take good care of the earth and its creatures (Gen. 1:26).

Humans can think and can plan the future; animals

follow their instincts. Human beings know right from wrong; animals just know how to survive. Humans communicate with language; animals can't use words.

Animals don't walk upright on two feet all day long the way humans do. They can't paint pictures or write music. Plus, if you watch your breath on a cold day, you'll see it float up toward the sky—but the breath of a sheep or a dog falls toward the ground. Those differences are some of God's hints that humans are distinct from the animals.

Pets are great, but they're not people. They don't reflect God's image, and he didn't put them in charge of things. Humans are the only creatures made in the image of God.

Reflection: Do you have a special pet? How is your pet a good companion to you? In what ways is an animal not able to be the kind of friend that a human being can be?

Prayer Point: *Thank you, God, for creating me with the ability to think, plan ahead, and use language. Help me be kind and responsible in the way I treat animals.*

Marvelously Made

"For you created my inmost being; you knit me together in my mother's womb. I praise you because I am fearfully and wonderfully made..." –Psalm 139:13-14

There's only one of you in this world, and it's a good thing you're here! God made you just the way he did on purpose. He delights in who you are, even on days when you're maybe not so very delighted in yourself (I'm sorry if you feel that way sometimes).

God decided whether you would be a girl or boy. He decided whether you would be short or tall, and whether you would most enjoy science or singing or soccer. He decided whether you would love being around people all day, or would rather hide away with a good book. He has special plans for you that aren't quite like his plans for anyone else.

You may not have learned a lot about human biology yet. But here's a really interesting thing: every time two special cells come together—one from a father and one from a mother—a brand new human being comes to life and starts to grow!

God brought you to life when you were so tiny it would have taken a powerful microscope to see you. He made you develop and grow to the size of a pea, then a bean, then a grape. You kept growing, and after about nine months, you were born.

God meant for you to be *you*, and not anyone else. You didn't start as something else and then become human. You've always been the person you are, even when you were too small to see.

Even though some people believe that God isn't real and human beings somehow happened by accident, God tells us in the Bible that he makes each one of us just the way we are *on purpose*—including you.

You are marvelously made.

Reflection: Do you sometimes wish God had made you a little differently than He did? Do you wish you were more like someone else at school or at church or in your neighborhood? Ask God to help you be happy that you are you. He sure is!

Prayer Point: *Lord, thank you that I'm not an accident. Thank you for making me just the way you want me to be. Help me to be glad that I'm me, and to remember I'm marvelously made.*

A Garden and a Snake

"'You will not certainly die,' the serpent said to the woman. 'For God knows that when you eat from it your eyes will be opened, and you will be like God, knowing good and evil.'" –Genesis 3:4-5

When God made the world, everything was perfect. The first people, Adam and Eve, took care of the animals and worked happily in a special place named the Garden of Eden. They were best friends with each other and with God.

God loved Adam and Eve very much. He only had one rule for them to follow. He commanded them not to eat the fruit from one certain tree in the garden.

Adam and Eve had an enemy who hated them because he hated God. Satan wished he could be the boss of everything. He was jealous of God. He wanted to ruin relationships between the humans and God.

One day, Satan pretended to be a snake. He tricked the humans into eating the fruit God had told them not to eat. They listened to Satan instead of trusting and obeying God. They took a bite.

All of a sudden, Adam and Eve felt ashamed and afraid. They hid from God. Because they disobeyed, God had to punish them by kicking them out of the special garden. That one bite was the first sin. It was the worst decision ever.

Work became hard instead of fun. Pain and sickness and

death came into the world. Animals started attacking and eating each other. In other words, the whole world became a broken place. You can tell it's still broken, right? Sad and hard things happen all the time.

But there's good news: even before things went so terribly wrong, God made a plan to fix everything.

Reflection: Have you ever gotten tricked into doing something you knew was wrong? How did you feel afterward? As a human being, you have a conscience that tells you right from wrong (Acts 24:16).

Prayer Point: *God, thank you for creating me with a conscience so I know what is right and what is wrong. Please give me the strength and wisdom to obey your commands.*

A Promise and a Plan

"For I do not do the good I want to do, but the evil I do not want to do—this I keep on doing. Now if I do what I do not want to do, it is no longer I who do it, but it is sin living in me that does it." –Romans 7:19-20

Have you ever tried hard to do the right thing, but failed? Ever since Adam and Eve made that horrible choice, all of us have had a huge problem. We have what the Bible calls a "sin nature." We disobey God, again and again.

God can't be near sin because he is perfect and holy. Our sin separates us from God. It's a big deal to him, and a big problem for us. Since we sin, how can we come close to a holy God and have friendship with him (Romans 5:12)?

God knew about this problem ahead of time. When the first humans disobeyed him and brought sin into the world, he already had a plan to rescue us. He promised he would send someone to save us from sin. But only someone perfect could pay the price for all the things we've done wrong. So who could that be?

Well, God sent his own Son to earth as a baby. Remember how you started out so small it would take a microscope to see you? Jesus started out as a human the same way. He was marvelously made as he grew deep inside his mother for nine months just like you did. But Jesus was different than you and me. He didn't have a human father. His Father is God, and Jesus is God, too.

That means Jesus was the only person in the world without the sin problem that the rest of us have. And that's really important, because only someone who could live perfectly would be able to rescue us from sin and selfishness (John 1:29).

Jesus, God's Son, would fulfill God's promise to rescue us from sin. But how?

Reflection: Have you ever tried really hard to do the right thing, but then you gave up because it's too hard? Do you ever do what is best for yourself instead of what is best for another person? That's because you have a sin nature.

Prayer Point: *God, I can see that I have a sin problem. Thank you for your perfect plan and your promise to rescue people from sin. Help me to understand how your promise rescues me.*

A Hero to the Rescue

"For even the Son of Man did not come to be served, but to serve, and to give his life as a ransom for many."
–Mark 10:45

Who is your favorite superhero? Superman? Wonder Woman? Spiderman? Maybe you've even made up a new superhero that isn't in the movies yet.

Everybody loves it when a superhero shows up just in time to save people in trouble. Well, in the days when Jesus walked the earth, the whole world had been in trouble for a long time. Everything was broken by sin.

People were unkind to each other. They treated poor people and sick people badly. They took things that didn't belong to them. They were proud and looked down on others. In other words, they kept choosing to be selfish instead of loving.

Jesus began to teach people about a different way to live. He called this new way of living the "kingdom of God." He did miracles like bringing a dead girl back to life and feeding a huge, hungry crowd with one boy's small lunch (Matthew 9:18-26; John 6:1-11).

Slowly, Jesus' followers understood more about God's plan to rescue human beings. They realized that Jesus was the special one who would rescue us from sin–the one God had promised.

But Jesus wasn't a flashy superhero who swooped in to rescue while everybody cheered. When Jesus came to earth, he quietly grew inside his mother, Mary. God crept into our world and put human skin on. We could learn what he is like without being scared away from him.

Jesus is the greatest hero in the best story ever, a story with some surprises.

Reflection: Jesus is the King of everything, but when he came to earth as a man, he came to serve us. What do you think serving means, and how can you serve other people like Jesus did?

Prayer Point: *Lord, help me notice when I have a chance to do things for other people. Help me to think about what others want and need, and how I can bless them.*

Better Than a Superhero

"This mystery is that through the gospel the Gentiles are... sharers together in the promise in Christ Jesus."
–Ephesians 3:6

Even though Jesus' followers slowly figured out he was the promised rescuer, they still had some wrong ideas of what he would rescue them from, and how we would do it.

People called Romans bullied their nation, Israel. The Romans didn't believe all humans bear God's image—they thought only their emperor did. ("Bear" means to carry or reflect.) So they thought it was okay to be bossy and mean to other groups of people.

Jesus' followers thought he would be the leader who would bring freedom to their people from the Romans. But Jesus had a much bigger job to do. He didn't just come to rescue one nation from another nation. He came to rescue all people everywhere from the power of sin.

This was not an easy job. The way it happened was very hard. Some proud, religious people lied about Jesus and blamed him for things he didn't do. They had him killed on a Roman cross—the worst possible way to die (Luke 23:33).

Jesus knew this would have to happen. He even begged his Father God to let him out of it somehow (Matthew 26:39). But there was no other way for us to be able to have friendship with God again. So Jesus said "yes" to the hard plan. He loves us that much. He loves *you* that much.

Here's how Jesus is far better than a superhero.

A superhero uses his or her special powers to help people, but they can only be in one place at a time. Superheroes rescue people from danger, but they can't rescue people from the problem inside of them—sin.

Jesus is real, not a pretend rescuer somebody made up. He is everywhere at once, so he is always with you—not only when you are in trouble. He doesn't just have one special power—he has ALL power (Ephesians 1:22)! Best of all, Jesus lived perfectly, so he was able to pay the price for everything we've done wrong.

Jesus is much more than a superhero. He is our Savior.

Reflection: Have you ever prayed for something, but then you didn't get the answer you hoped for? Sometimes God has a bigger plan in mind.

Prayer Point: *Lord, I know you are great and much wiser than I am. Help me to remember that I can trust you when you don't answer my prayers the way I want you to.*

The Best News Ever

"'He is not here; he has risen, just as he said. Come and see the place where he lay.'" –Matthew 28:6

When Jesus died, his followers were very sad, confused and scared. Now who would teach them and lead them? Who would rescue them from the Romans? They still didn't understand why things happened the way they did.

Three days after he died, Jesus came back to life. Death could not keep him in the grave! Jesus' resurrection proves he is the Son of God and King over everything.

Jesus is the only person who chose love over selfishness, every single time. Not only did he pay for our sins … he also made it possible for us to live with God forever (Romans 6:23).

Remember how the first humans, Adam and Eve, had a perfect friendship with God in the beginning? Well, Jesus made it possible for us to have a friendship with God again—one that lasts forever. He made it possible for us to be adopted into God's family (Galatians 4:6).

You can have that kind of friendship with God by trusting in Jesus to rescue you (Romans 10:9). The story of how Jesus saves us is called the gospel (which means "good news"). The message of the gospel starts with bad news and ends with good news.

We could put the gospel message this way: *You are more broken than you know, and more loved than you could ever imagine.*

First, we have to agree that we are broken. Only then are we ready to receive God's love. To bring the gospel message home to your heart, agree with God that you have disobeyed him. Thank him for sending Jesus to rescue you from sin. Tell him you want to be part of his family and have a friendship with him forever.

What happens next will change everything.

Reflection: Maybe you already understand the gospel and you already have a friendship with Jesus. If so, that's wonderful! If not, you can pray and receive Jesus' plan to rescue you right now.

Prayer Point: *Lord Jesus, I agree that I am broken inside. I know I have disobeyed you and I don't have the power to change myself. Thank you for loving me so much that you died to pay for all my selfishness and the ways I've messed up. I trust you to rescue me from sin and be my Lord and friend forever.*

Day 9

A New Creation

"Therefore, if anyone is in Christ, the new creation has come: The old has gone, the new is here!"
–2 Corinthians 5:17

When I was a kid, my brother and I caught a bunch of tadpoles and put them in a pond in our yard. In a few weeks, their tails disappeared, they grew legs, and their gills changed to lungs. They weren't tadpoles anymore; they were frogs! It's pretty crazy that a creature can start out looking like one thing and then turn into something so very different.

That's exactly what happens to people who choose to love and follow Jesus. Just like tadpoles turn into frogs or caterpillars turn into butterflies, when you put your trust in Jesus, he transforms—or completely changes—you.

Here's what this *doesn't* mean: you will be perfect from now on, and you will never mess up again. It *does* mean that now, you will be able to obey God. He will give you the power to do it.

Before you make a choice to follow Jesus and trust in his rescue plan, the Bible says you are actually trapped into making sinful, selfish choices. You think and say and do wrong things because you don't have the power to do good, even when you want to do it (Romans 7:19).

But once you trust in Jesus and obey him as your Lord, he gives you the power to say no to sin and do the right thing.

Now you have a choice, because his Holy Spirit lives inside you and gives you strength to obey (Romans 8:1-2). You get to pick the right thing, the brave and kind thing, the unselfish thing, because you belong to Jesus!

That's great news. It means you'll be able to show brave love to others, even when it's hard—because God is at work changing you.

Reflection: Jesus is the only person in the world who, for his whole earthly life, always chose loving others over being selfish. Now that you are a follower of Jesus, the Holy Spirit gives you the power to be like him!

Prayer Point: *Lord Jesus, thank you that you have made me a new creation. Help me to remember you have given me the power to be like you in the way I treat others.*

The Grand Story of God

"Give thanks to the Lord, for he is good;
his love endures forever." –I Chronicles 16:34

You may have heard folks say that people are basically good. They think if we work hard enough, we can fix the world without God's help. Some people don't even believe there is a God. They think living things got here by accident, and that human beings are merely a type of animal.

That's not what the Bible tells us (Psalm 14:3).

God's story is the best and truest story of all. He says human beings were made in his image. We were created to reflect him in a special way, unlike the animals, and to be in charge of things for him. But his image in us is broken because of sin. So we reflect God in bits and pieces like a cracked mirror.

You've learned the good news about the only one who can rescue us – God's Son, Jesus. When you decide to trust in Jesus as your Savior. God begins to transform you. So God not only created you in the first place—now he's transforming you (2 Corinthians 3:18).

What is he turning you into? He's making you more and more like Jesus in your words, attitudes and actions. Jesus reflected God perfectly, and now God is healing all the cracks and broken places in you so you can reflect God clearly to the world, too.

Because of sin, people are *not* basically good. We're born

selfish. But the good news? We can be rescued from our sinful, selfish ways and become part of God's family forever.

God *is* good, and we have an important part in his story. You may think of yourself as just a kid—but you have a special part in God's story that no one else does.

Reflection: Do you think people are basically good, or basically selfish? Why or why not?

Prayer Point: *Lord, thank you that you are completely good and that we can trust you all the way. Help me to understand your grand story and how everything fits together and makes sense when I trust and believe you.*

Section Reflection: Made in God's Image

You've been reading in this book about how people were created to reflect God. You've learned that God loves people so much he developed a plan to rescue us after sin invaded the world. The plan caused him pain, but he thought it was well worth it because he loves us so much.

You are very valuable to God! He is glad about you. He's especially glad if you've made the decision to trust Jesus as your rescuer—your Savior. That means he gets to enjoy having you in his family forever.

There's something else you should know.

This grand story you've been learning about is a love story. I'm not talking about the mushy kind. I'm talking about a love story between God and his people—a story that helps *us* love people, too.

As a human being, you are created in God's image. However, because of sin, you can only reflect his image in bits and pieces. When you trust Jesus as your rescuer, he fixes the broken places in you so you become more and more like him. As you become more like Jesus, you will reflect at least one quality of God's character.

You will reflect his love.

Part 2

Broken but Beautiful

"And we all, who with unveiled faces contemplate the Lord's glory, are being transformed into his image with ever-increasing glory, which comes from the Lord, who is the Spirit."

– 2 Corinthians 3:18

When the Earth is Made New

"The wolf will live with the lamb, the leopard will lie down with the goat, the calf and the lion and the yearling together; and a little child will lead them." –Isaiah 11:6

Have you ever seen a cat catch a mouse and eat it? Pretty gross, right? As much as I enjoy my kitties, I really don't like some of their eating habits.

Good news: one day, cats won't eat mice anymore. Wolves won't kill caribou. Sharks won't eat seals. Tigers won't pounce on humans.

In the Garden of Eden, God promised to send a rescuer to save us. And he did. God also made another promise. He said that one day, our rescuer will return a second time to make everything new (Hebrews 9:28).

Jesus is not only *our* rescuer, but what he did to save people will restore the whole creation, making it perfect as it was before. Those who trust in Jesus as their Savior will enjoy a new earth with no more pain, sickness or dying. There will be no more earthquakes, tsunamis or hurricanes. God will wipe away all our tears and we will be happy with him forever (Revelation 21:4).

Imagine a snow-white lamb taking a nap between the huge paws of a lion. Imagine a fawn playing leapfrog with a cougar, or a bunny touching twitchy noses with a fox.

When God first created the world and enjoyed friendship

with humans, everything was peaceful and perfect like that. One day, it will be again.

The hard part is that it's plain to see things are still broken right now. Cats still eat mice. We still have earthquakes and tornadoes. Even worse than that, people are still selfish and mean to each other.

We still have a sin problem in our world. So how does God's grand story mend people's hearts right now? And how can you play a part?

Reflection: Some people say if there is a God and he is good, bad things wouldn't happen. But sin broke our world and God will restore it one day. How does knowing this help you trust God?

Prayer Point: *Lord Jesus, thank you for the wonderful hope I have as your follower. Please give me wisdom so I can help others understand your goodness and your perfect plan.*

Good News, Bad News

"The Lord is not slow in keeping his promise.... Instead he is patient with you, not wanting anyone to perish, but everyone to come to repentance." –2 Peter 3:9

Gospel means good news—the good news about Jesus. Those of us who trust in Jesus to be rescued from sin and selfishness have the power to stop sinning and be like him. One day, we'll live in a world that's been made brand-new again.

But what happens to those who *don't* trust in Jesus?

Well, the good news about Jesus starts with the bad news about people. People are sinners. We do wrong, selfish things. We mess up, again and again. Since God is holy and just, sin cannot be near him. Somebody needed to pay for our sin so we could have friendship with God again. That someone was Jesus.

Does Jesus' sacrifice automatically rescue everyone from sin and its consequences? No.

Imagine a man falling overboard from a ship into the deep ocean. A crew member grabs a life preserver and tosses it to the drowning man. If the struggling swimmer ignores the life preserver, he will drown, even though the rescuer made it possible for him to be saved.

Not everybody in the world is a friend of God's and goes to heaven. Each person must make their own choice to receive the gift of salvation to be rescued (John 3:16-18).

If not, they will go to a place God created for punishing Satan. It's a miserable, lonely, awful place–and it lasts forever, just like heaven (Mark 9:47-49). They will be completely cut off from God (2 Thessalonians 1:9). The chance to accept his offer of rescue has an end.

This bad news is the reason we must show brave love to others and tell them the good news of Jesus. He doesn't want anyone to miss out on the chance to choose a wonderful life that lasts forever.

Reflection: God didn't create hell for humans, and he doesn't want any humans to go there. He lets them choose a forever that's with him or without him. Talk with your parents or another adult about how you might be able to help others think wisely about where they will spend forever.

Prayer Point: *Lord, help me to show brave love to people who don't believe in you yet. Give me the words to say or the questions to ask to help them start thinking right thoughts about you.*

How Christians Mend the World

"He told them another parable: 'The kingdom of heaven is like a mustard seed, which a man took and planted in his field. Though it is the smallest of all seeds, yet when it grows, it is the largest of garden plants and becomes a tree, so that the birds come and perch in its branches.'"
–Matthew 13:31-32

Jesus taught that real change comes from the inside out. He used word pictures to explain this. Like the way a small amount of yeast makes a whole loaf of bread rise. Or the way a tiny seed grows into a huge tree.

The more we get to know God and the Bible, the more we can plant good seeds in the lives of other people. We can reflect his love to them so they can come to know him, too. And we cause good changes to happen in the world because we value other people as God's image bearers.

Did you know that, for thousands of years, most people in the world were poor and never went to school? Many were slaves, and women didn't have any rights. No hospitals or public schools existed. No one cared for babies born with health problems. They were abandoned, left out in the fields to die.

Guess who started the idea of adoption? Christians! Guess who influenced governments to outlaw slavery and started setting up hospitals for sick people and schooling for all children? You guessed it—Christians! The spread of Christianity caused all kinds of good changes like these.

Many people don't know this. They think everyone has always known people should love each other. But for most of human history, people and nations fought for power over each other. It was all about honor or shame, not love. It's because of Jesus we now understand we should love each other.

Find ways to share the love of Jesus with other people. Start with believing God deeply loves and values you, the way you are. When you truly believe that, you can help others understand God loves and values them, too.

Reflection: Did you know Christians started many good things like schooling for every child, adoption for unwanted babies, hospitals for sick people, and freedom for slaves? Spend a few minutes thinking about how brave love really does change the world.

Prayer Point: *Lord Jesus, thank you that following you means so much good happens for so many people. Help me follow you closely so that my brave love can help change the world, too.*

You are God's Masterpiece

"For we are God's handiwork, created in Christ Jesus to do good works, which God prepared in advance for us to do." –Ephesians 2:10

Do you have a favorite creative activity, such as drawing, writing or dancing? Whenever humans make or design something artistic, they demonstrate they're made in the image of the One who created everything.

Near where I live, there's a town called Joseph. On a warm summer day, I like to walk up and down the main street in Joseph to see the life-sized bronze sculptures on almost every corner.

These masterpiece sculptures include a cowboy riding a wild bronco, a woman in a long, flowing dress and sunhat, and a puma sneaking over a boulder. There's an eagle, two wolves running, and the famous chief of the Nez Perce people, Chief Joseph.

Many people enjoy looking at these excellent pieces of art, as well as beautiful paintings for sale in the art shops in town.

Did you know you are a masterpiece, too? As an image-bearer of God, you are like a poem he is writing, or a picture he is painting. He's working on you the way a potter molds a spinning piece of clay on his wheel (Isaiah 64:8).

God shows the world something about himself through you. Also, he's not finished working on you. You need to know this on days when life is hard.

You matter very much to God. Other people matter to him, too. When you're convinced of these two truths, you'll have courage to witness about God's love, so others can also become a part of his family.

Reflection: Did you know God is carefully working on you like an artist works on his finest painting, or a writer works on her best book? How does knowing that make you feel?

Prayer Point: *Lord, you are the Master Artist who does all things well. Thank you for your good work in my life as you shape me into a masterpiece.*

Day 15

Don't Use the Wrong Glasses

"Are not five sparrows sold for two pennies? Yet not one of them is forgotten by God. Indeed, the very hairs of your head are all numbered. Don't be afraid; you are worth more than many sparrows." –Luke 12:6-7

My grandchildren love to play with glasses. If they see my reading glasses lying around, they put them on and pretend to be grown-ups. However, the only thing reading glasses do for a toddler is to make the world look fuzzy!

That's kind of how it is when we look at people differently than the way God looks at them. Remember, God sees his own image in every person, and he made each person the way they are on purpose. But we often make the mistake of comparing ourselves to each other. We act like the best person is the one who is the smartest or the prettiest or the strongest.

This creates a huge problem.

If we base our value on what other people think of us instead of what God thinks of us, we might see ourselves as losers instead of valuable, one-of-a-kind image-bearers of God. That's really sad—and it's not true at all!

The other problem is that if we base other people's value on what everybody thinks instead of what God says, we'll make other people feel like losers, too. It's kind of a no-win deal.

It's super important to remember that God loves and values every single person. He doesn't compare us to anyone else. He thinks every one of us is amazing – and what God thinks is what is true.

So when you think about yourself, don't put on the wrong glasses. Don't buy the lie that you aren't good enough. You are exactly who you are supposed to be. No one else in the world can take your place.

God cares about you so much that he counts how many hairs are on your head (Matthew 10:30)!

Reflection: We can be tempted to think too little or too much of ourselves. Either way, we are being self-focused. We're using the wrong glasses. When you compare yourself to others, how do those "wrong glasses" make your focus fuzzy?

Prayer Point: *Father, help me remember that what you think of me is what matters, because that's what is true—not what other people might think.*

How God helps us Reflect Him

"And we all, who with unveiled faces contemplate the Lord's glory, are being transformed into his image with ever-increasing glory, which comes from the Lord, who is the Spirit." – 2 Corinthians 3:18

My dad grew up in Germany, where he learned how to make beautiful wooden furniture. He also restored furniture which was old, dull, and beaten up.

Papa explained the steps of restoration to me. First, he said, you have to strip the piece down to its original surface. Remove every bit of the old varnish on it. Then you sand it fine and smooth. Finally, you apply a fresh coat of varnish, but you have to be super careful. You can't allow even a speck of dust to fall into the fresh surface, or it would get stuck and ruin it.

My dad knew how to take a piece of old beaten up furniture and make it look brand new again. When he was finished stripping, sanding, and carefully putting fresh varnish on the surface, he could look at the wood and see his own reflection in it.

That's how God is with you and me. He accepts us with all our imperfections and makes us what we were meant to be in the first place—his image-bearers. Just like an old table which has gotten dull, dented, and ugly, our sin and selfishness dull God's image in us and make it impossible for us to reflect him. But God knows how to strip, sand, and re-polish us. His work in our hearts makes it possible for him to see his reflection in us once again.

When you do something wrong and you feel guilty about it, that's actually the kindness of God at work (Romans 2:4). He's stripping and sanding you down so he can see himself reflected in your life. He's not doing this to be mean. He loves you and wants to make you more like Jesus. He's increasing the glory in you. (We'll talk more about what glory means on Day 18.)

While Jesus transforms you, he wants to show you the beauty in all people he created. Each of them is marvelously made.

Reflection: Can you think of a time when God lovingly corrected you or let you feel real guilt, so you could turn to him and be changed? Think about your feelings before and after this happened.

Prayer Point: *Father, thank you for loving me so much you don't leave me the way I am. Thank you for taking me from one level of glory to the next as you restore your image—your reflection—in me.*

God is a Collector

"'All that the Father gives me will come to me, and whoever comes to me I will never cast out'"
–John 6:37 (ESV)

Up the hill not far from where I live, there was once a huge junkyard surrounded by a cyclone fence. Everything from junked cars to random pieces of rusty scrap metal filled the property from one end to the other.

When someone finally bought the property and cleaned it up, they found all kinds of crazy things in the junk—even dangerous sticks of old dynamite! Most of the stuff ended up being hauled away. Thankfully, nothing blew up.

Collectors are different than junkyard owners. As a kid, my husband collected stamps, coins, and baseball cards. Collectors don't keep things because they don't know how to get rid of garbage; they collect because they see beauty and value in specific items.

When it comes to human beings, God is more like a collector than a junkyard owner. He sees value in us. He doesn't leave us lying around broken like all that stuff in the junkyard. He fixes the broken places in us. He never sees any of us as useless or not worth bothering with.

In God's eyes, there's no such thing as garbage when it comes to his image-bearers. He made us, so he knows how much we are worth. That's good news! God never looks at any of us and thinks, “Well, I guess I’ll toss that one onto the junk pile.”

God sees you as a treasure (Psalm 17:8). He also views the people around you as treasures. He wants to help you see them that way, too. That’s part of what it means to reflect God’s image.

Reflection: Can you think of someone who is hard to love (or maybe even hard to like)? How does knowing God sees them as a treasure help you not give up on showing love to them?

Prayer Point: *Lord Jesus, please help me to love people the way you do, and to never give up on them.*

What Does "Glory" Mean?

"You have made them a little lower than the angels, and crowned them with glory and honor." –Psalm 8:5

One evening, I sat in a café where a band played music. A few boys and girls danced in the middle of the floor. The waitress smiled as she poured coffee to people who talked and laughed at their tables.

Suddenly, I noticed the amazing beauty in every single person in the room. I could see them the way Jesus sees them. I felt like laughing with joy and crying at the same time, because my heart was so happy. There was nothing unusual about that crowd on that day. God chose the moment to allow me to see people the way he does—as ones who reflect his glory.

The New Testament part of the Bible was written mostly in ancient Greek. In Greek, the word we translate as glory is *doxa,* which means a special kind of splendor, honor, and beauty God has given to humans because we are somehow like him. This glory gradually increases in those who love and follow Jesus, because he is making us more like him (2 Corinthians 3:18). So we shine with human glory, but also with God's glory—a double dose of "doxa!"

Maybe you've run outside to see a beautiful sunset, and you've looked at the sky and whispered, "Wow!" That's kind of what it's like to notice the glory of people. C.S. Lewis, who wrote *The Chronicles of Narnia*, also authored a book called *The Weight of Glory*, in which he said, "There are no ordinary people." God created us below the angels—powerful spiritual beings who worship God, protect human beings, and announce special messages from God (see Daniel 9:21 and Luke 1:19). That's pretty cool!

Did you know Christians have a very high view of human beings? People who don't believe the Bible may believe human beings don't matter very much. After all, if we got here by accident, and there's no God who cares about us, how could human beings share his glory?

God sometimes surprises us in the Bible with a glimpse of how he looks at all of us. Those wonder moments help us realize how much God values each one of his image-bearers. Each of us reflects God's glory, and God wants us to find the beauty in others.

Reflection: Have you ever experienced an occasion where you realized every person around you is a lovely, wonderful, glorious creation? If not, ask God to give you moments like that.

Prayer Point: *Lord, open my eyes to see people the way you do, and fill my heart with your joy and love toward others.*

Cracked Mirrors

"'The Lord does not look at the things people look at. People look at the outward appearance, but the Lord looks at the heart.'" –1 Samuel 16:7

Since our world is broken by sin, human beings often don't see things clearly the way God sees things. We're all like broken mirrors which reflect God in bits and pieces. So instead of seeing how beautiful every person is, we think that certain people are attractive, but others are not. We tend to play favorites, but God doesn't.

We're tempted to hang out with popular people or be friends with someone who wears the right clothes or acts cool. We tend to avoid certain people because we're afraid if we spend time with them, others will think less of us.

Jesus made a point of seeking out the very people others pushed to the edges. He wanted to reach the ones who didn't have it all together. Jesus' words and actions made it plain that every human being has equal value in his eyes.

Jesus went to dinner at one tax collector's house, and invited another one to be his disciple, even though Jewish people hated tax collectors (Mark 2:13-17). He talked to women and spent time with them, even though other Jewish teachers ignored women and treated them as less valuable than men. He even healed a woman on the Sabbath, which was against the teachers' rules (Luke 13:16).

Jesus touched sick people others avoided (Matthew 8:1-3). He spent time with children and blessed them, even though his disciples thought he was too busy to bother with kids (Matthew 18:13-15). Again and again, Jesus, God's Son, showed us how much he values all people by seeking out the ones who matter least in some eyes.

Jesus is our example. We, too, need to notice and love the people everyone else ignores or avoids. We need to ask God for eyes to see people the way he does, and a heart full of brave love for them.

Reflection: When you're with your friends, do you find it hard to help a new person feel included in the group? Think of someone you know who isn't considered cool. Ask God how you can treat them the way Jesus would.

Prayer Point: *Lord, thank you for being my example in reaching out to people whom others would leave out. Please help me be more concerned about accepting others than I am about looking cool.*

Be Kind, but not Nice

"Be kind to one another, tenderhearted, forgiving one another, as God in Christ forgave you." –Ephesians 4:32

I often hear parents and grandparents telling their kids or grandkids, "Be nice." Did you know the Bible never tells us to be nice? God tells us to be kind and compassionate to one another. He tells us to be gentle in the way we explain the truth. But he never commands us to "be nice."

To be nice means to be agreeable and pleasant. You do what others want you to do. Sometimes that can be a good thing. For example, when you clean your room because your parents instruct you to, that's appropriate behavior. However, when someone wants you to tell a lie, or steal something, or put down other people, then going along with them is a bad thing.

Jesus always showed love and kindness, even when he was stern. He wanted what was best for us. Sometimes that includes speaking a hard truth. But Jesus was not "nice." He did not go along with other people's ideas of what he should be saying or doing.

The religious leaders thought Jesus shouldn't heal people on the Sabbath because it was against their rules. Jesus kept right on healing people (Mark 3:1-6). Jesus' brothers said he should tell everyone he was the Messiah. That's not the way God wanted people to find out. Pontius Pilate, the Roman governor who gave the order for Jesus to be crucified, wanted

Jesus to defend himself by answering certain questions. Jesus wouldn't answer him (Matthew 27:13-14).

Jesus is our example, and he wasn't merely nice. Instead, he showed kindness and brave love for the whole world, including the unwanted people.

Reflection: Think of a time when others wanted you to do something you knew wasn't right. Maybe it was breaking your mom or dad's rules, or doing something dangerous and foolish. Did you go along with it (niceness), or did you tell them you wouldn't because it's wrong (kindness)? Kindness takes more courage than niceness!

Prayer Point: *Lord Jesus, thank you for showing me what real kindness looks like. Help me be boldly loving, not just agreeable, in the way I treat others.*

Section Reflection: Broken but Beautiful

God will restore his world one day. Only those who receive the gift of rescue offered by Jesus will get to live there after they die. Or when Jesus comes back to rule the earth, which he promised he will do.

Christians have made lots of good changes in our broken world because they have the love of Jesus in their heart toward others. Even though the world is broken, we don't give up on people. We bring God's love to them.

You are a treasure to God, so don't look at yourself through the wrong glasses. You are God's masterpiece, like a painting or a poem. He is proud of you—and he's not done with you yet. He's making it possible for his reflection (his image) to be seen clearly in you.

One of the ways God works in you is by giving the ability to see people the way he does. He wants you to see the amazing beauty in all people, something he calls *glory*. He especially wants you to notice and care about the people everyone else seems to stay away from.

In order to show God's love, you need a brave heart. It's not about being nice and trying to please everybody. It's about being strong and kind, and doing what is right.

In the next section, we'll learn more about how to be brave and kind, especially toward people who have been put down, picked on, and pushed aside by others.

Keep in mind that being brave doesn't mean being foolish. Real bravery includes wisdom. Your parents, and other adult Christians, can help you reach out to others in wise and safe ways.

Part 3

Pushed-Aside People

"The King will reply, 'Truly I tell you, whatever you did for one of the least of these brothers and sisters of mine, you did for me.'"

–Matthew 25:40

Day 21

Some Things Should Make You Mad

"God is a righteous judge, and a God who feels indignation every day." –Psalm 7:11 (ESV)

One day during my sixth grade year, out on the playground, a group of girls chose one of those large, rubber balls for a game of foursquare. Then a group of mean boys snatched the ball away and started playing with it. One girl came to me and said, "Those boys took our ball."

I didn't feel like the bravest girl on the playground. If those boys had taken a ball away from me, I probably would have stood there and done nothing. But somehow, because someone else needed help, I felt braver.

I marched over to the boys, grabbed the ball, and gave it back to the girls. The surprised boys didn't argue. I saved recess that day, and it felt good!

Have you ever felt angry because of a mean act done to someone else? This feeling comes from God. He made us with a sense of *justice* (Isaiah 1:17).

God is holy, just and righteous. He wants us to treat each other justly (Micah 6:8). We can't take things from others or put them down or act like we are better than they are. We should stand up for those who are being bullied.

Did you know Jesus got really mad sometimes?

The temple was supposed to be God's house, but lots of people emphasized making money by selling things to others at high prices, instead of worshipping God. One day, Jesus entered the temple, flipped over the seller's tables, and yelled at them for turning his Father God's house into a place where people got ripped off (John 2:14-16)!

Now, Jesus' anger was never selfish or foolish. But ours often is. We have to be careful about our anger. We need to ask God—and maybe a parent or another wise adult—what to do with it. (Hint: When we see bullying, usually the best way to help is to go tell an adult.)

When you see wrong things done to other people and you feel angry about it, your anger makes sense. As God's image-bearer, you reflect his desire for justice.

Reflection: Think about a time when you saw someone do something wrong to another person. Did you feel angry? If so, what did you do with your anger?

Prayer Point: *Father, thank you that you are a just God. Help me to be wise when I feel angry about wrong things, and to remember to ask you (and wise adults) what to do.*

Different Doesn't Mean Worth Less

"The Lord said to (Moses), 'Who gave human beings their mouths? Who makes them deaf or mute? Who gives them sight or makes them blind? Is it not I, the Lord?'"
– Exodus 4:11

Can you imagine being born with no arms and only one small part of a leg? That's what happened to a man named Nick Vujicic.

From birth, ordinary things proved hard for Nick to do. On top of that, kids at school bullied him. By the time he was eight years old, Nick became so depressed he tried to drown himself.

Then Nick's mom showed him a newspaper article about a man who also had a severe disability. Nick began to think about how he could help other people. He decided to accept his life the way it was and to look for ways to be kind and helpful.

Today, Nick travels all over the world speaking to thousands of people. He tells them not to believe the lie that they are worthless. He tells them God loves them and created them for a reason.

Nick can walk, swim and surf. He is married and has two children. Nick has hope in his heart because he knows God makes beautiful things out of the challenges in our lives.

Our enemy, the devil, tried to convince Nick he lacked worth more than everybody else. If Nick had believed that lie, he might not be here today. He wouldn't be able to help so many.

Even though he doesn't have arms or legs, Nick is still a beautiful image-bearer of God. He has a heart full of love. God shows people things about themselves through Nick. His life points others to Jesus.

Reflection: Do you know someone who looks or acts differently from most other people? Perhaps they are disabled in some way, either in body or mind. How can you encourage them today?

____

____

____

____

____

____

____

____

____

____

____

____

Prayer Point: *Lord, help me to be kind and encouraging to those who are different than me. Help me to see how valuable they are, and help me not be afraid to talk to them.*

It's Not about Houses and Money

"Then he said to them, 'Watch out! Be on your guard against all kinds of greed; life does not consist in an abundance of possessions.'"–Luke 12:15

As a student in Bible college, I joined a drama group. We moved to a big city for the summer and did short plays outdoors about the good news of Jesus.

Some days, we would set up in the city park. Many who watched us perform actually lived in the park. They had no homes of their own, so they slept on benches or underneath bushes. They didn't own much; mostly the clothes they wore.

We had really interesting conversations with the park people. Once, one of the men came right into one of our plays as if he was one of the actors! Some of the people we met were mentally ill. Some were sick. Or hooked on drugs or alcohol. All had gone through hard times which prevented paying for a house or apartment.

Sadly, people blessed with homes and jobs often look down on homeless men and women. They think not having a home is their own fault. But sometimes people lose their money and their homes even if they work hard. Either way, God doesn't value people more or less based on where they live or how much money they possess (1 Samuel 16:7).

In the town where we live now, my husband was running on an exercise path when he noticed mean words about homeless people spray-painted on the path. This made him angry. He called the police and asked them to remove those words.

It's not okay to say terrible things about people because they don't have a place to live. It's not okay to think less of others when they don't have what we do (Romans 12:16).

Have you ever seen a person sitting on a city street corner holding a cardboard sign that says they need money? That person is an image-bearer of God. He or she has dignity and worth in God's eyes, and we should not look down on them.

Reflection: Think about what it would be like to have to move out of your home and sleep under a bridge or in a cardboard box. You would not be able to fix your own food or take a shower. How would that feel?

Prayer Point: *Lord, thank you for the roof over my head, the clothes I have to wear, and the food I have to eat. Please help me think kindly toward those who have less than I do. Show me how I might be able to help them in a way that is safe and wise.*

Every Nation, Tribe and Language

"...before me was a great multitude that no one could count, from every nation, tribe, people and language, standing before the throne and before the Lamb"
–Revelation 7:9

The Bible tells us God created all kinds of people groups in the world. He made groups of image-bearers who speak various languages and have different looks. He loves this beautiful variety in the human beings he created (Deuteronomy 10:17-19).

However, since our world is broken by sin, people from various countries and races fight for power over one another. Some nations push other nations off their land. They force people from other nations to be their slaves. Some nation's leaders have killed thousands or even millions of certain kinds of people because they weren't part of their own people group. They wanted to get rid of them.

Some people groups enjoy more privileges, such as chances to get good jobs. When this feels unfair, some try to get back at those who have more opportunities. This causes problems, too.

Injustice causes awkwardness and hard feelings between people of different races. They may not trust each other. We can't change what happened in the past, but it's important to understand what still bothers whole groups of human beings.

Perhaps you know someone who is from another country or is of a different race (has a different skin color) than yours.

Ask good questions. Listen to your friend. Show that you value them as God's image-bearer. What is his or her family life like? What traditions do they have? What do they hope to do when they grow up?

God is very creative. He made people with many skin tones, face shapes and body types. All of them reflect his image, and are equally important to him.

Reflection: Do you have friends who speak another language or are of a different race than yours? Think about how you can try to put yourself in their shoes to understand them better.

Prayer Point: *Father, thank you for creating so many interesting and beautiful kinds of image-bearers. Help me appreciate those differences and be willing to learn about other groups of people besides my own.*

Temples, Synagogues and Mosques

"From one man he made all the nations, that they should inhabit the whole earth; and he marked out their appointed times in history and the boundaries of their lands. God did this so that they would seek him and perhaps reach out for him and find him..."
–Acts 17:26-27

When I was in high school, a Jewish friend invited me to his family's house for a Passover meal. I knew about Passover from reading the book of Exodus and other parts of the Bible, but for the first time I ate a Passover meal with a Jewish family.

The evening was fun and interesting, and it gave me more chances to talk to my friend about Jesus. The Bible describes Jesus as the Lamb who died for our sins, and that is what Passover is really all about.

I had another friend who attended the local Latter Day Saints (Mormon) Church. I wanted her to know more about Jesus, too, so we decided to take turns going to each other's churches. I went to hers once, and she went to mine.

You might know a family who is Muslim, and maybe the women wear veils. You might know someone who is Buddhist. Or maybe you know someone who doesn't belong to any religion because they think God isn't real.

The good news is that Jesus is for everyone! It doesn't matter how much they do or don't understand about him yet—he loves them, and he wants them to come to know him. But as we share the good news about Jesus, who he is and why we need him, we need God's wisdom in how we do that.

Many people think you can believe whatever you want, but that you shouldn't tell others your belief is what's really true. They think all religions are pretty much the same. They make it sound like it's prideful to believe Jesus is the only way to God. But Jesus himself said this, and that's how we know it's true (John 14:6).

It's actually humble to put our faith in Jesus alone! When we have a forever friendship with God, we realize how much we needed Jesus to rescue us, and that no one else could do it.

Jesus wants to rescue every beautiful image-bearer created by God.

Reflection: Do you know any neighbors or other people who don't believe the same way you do? How can you learn about what they believe and look for chances to tell them about Jesus? Your parents or an adult from church may be able to help you have these conversations in a wise way.

___

___

___

___

___

___

___

___

___

___

___

Prayer Point: *Father, thank you for your great love for all people, no matter what they think or believe about you. Help me learn about other beliefs in a humble way, and help me show brave love in talking about Jesus.*

Should I Be a Boy or a Girl?

"For God is not a God of confusion but of peace."
– 1 Corinthians 14:33 (ESV)

When I was in high school, we performed musical plays once a year. One year, a small, quiet, 10th grade boy got the lead role in the musical.

Up until that time, no one noticed this boy. Not big enough to play football, he wasn't one of the popular guys. But as soon as this boy began to sing, we all heard the deep, rich voice God gave him. All of a sudden everybody wanted to hang out with him!

Some boys are good at things that might not seem manly. Some girls excel at non-girly activities. That's okay! Girls or boys should do what they like and can do well. Enjoying non-typical activities doesn't indicate a person was born with the wrong body.

When God created humans, he made them male and female on purpose, and he said this was very good (Genesis 1:31). But people can get confused, because they don't know what the Bible says. Or they don't believe it. They think children should decide whether to be a boy or girl based on how they feel instead of based on the body God gave them. However, our feelings can lie to us, and they can change.

It's important to follow God's truth and agree he didn't make mistakes in the way he created us. Be especially kind to boys and girls who feel confused about this. It's a very hard thing for them.

If you know a girl or boy who feels mixed up about who they are, or whether they should like other boys or other girls, you can show brave love to them. You can stand up for them if others make fun of them or bully them. You can show them you love them the way they are. And so does Jesus.

Every girl and boy is a beautiful image-bearer of God, and our human bodies are a good gift from God. And when we follow Jesus, our body becomes a temple where the Holy Spirit lives (Corinthians 6:19-20).

Reflection: Think about what it would be like to feel confused about your body and who you should like. (Maybe you do feel a little mixed up and unsure, so you know how it feels.) Can you see how this would be a very hard thing, since people get bullied for it?

___

___

___

___

___

___

___

___

___

___

___

Prayer Point: *Lord, thank you for the good gift of the body you gave me. Please help me always be grateful for this good gift, and to be kind to those who may feel confused in this area.*

Are Some People Useless?

"But I trust in you, Lord; I say, 'You are my God. My times are in your hands…'" –Psalm 31:14-15

I know a lady named Barb whose college-student daughter Katie survived a bad car accident. Afterward, Katie couldn't move by herself or talk. She had to lie in a special bed and be cared for all the time.

Katie lived for many years after the accident. It was hard to take care of her, and it cost lots of money. But when Katie died, her mom and many other people were very sad and missed her a lot. That's because Katie was important. She was an image-bearer of God. She didn't have to do anything to prove that. People loved her because she was Katie.

Some think people like Katie don't have a right to be alive. They think we should get rid of people who are too sick or injured to care for themselves, or can't talk. They measure a person's worth by what they can do. But God says we have value because we are made in his image.

What if someone is so sick or feels so hopeless they want to die? Should we help them end their lives?

Helping suffering people die might sound like kindness, but it's not. It's like trying to be God. When we start playing around with the idea of helping people die, it leads to trouble.

Humans have a sin nature. Sin tempts us to want power over others.

Image-bearers belong to God. He created us. He loves us. Our lives, including the timing of our deaths, belong in his hands (Psalm 31:14-15).

Reflection: Do you know anyone who can't get around and do things, or who can't talk like most people? How can you show that person love and respect?

Prayer Point: *Lord, thank you that our times are in your hand. Help me show sick, injured or sad people that they have value and they can trust you with their lives.*

older Means Wiser, not Worthless

"Gray hair is a crown of splendor; it is attained in the way of righteousness." –Proverbs 16:31

When I was in fourth grade, my dad cared for elderly people as a business. He managed a home of forty people, and my brothers and sister and I got to know many of them. Some of these folks neared a hundred years old! They had some really interesting stories to tell.

One lady told us what it was like during the big earthquake way back in 1906. Others told us stories about a time when hardly anyone owned a car.

Getting old is a hard thing. People's bodies slow down and they can't get around as well. Their hearing, eyesight and memory might get worse. They may not be able to drive anymore, or go to as many places. They can't work or play as well as they used to.

Does that mean older people are worth less than younger people? No. Senior citizens still bear God's beautiful image, no matter how bent and wrinkled they may look, or despite what they can or can't do.

Also, older people have seen events and lived through experiences that others don't know about. They have lived more years than we have, which means they've had a chance to grow in wisdom (Job 12:12).

God commands us to show honor and respect to older

people (Leviticus 19:32). He sees value in every one of his image-bearers, from the beginning to end of life. You can show you value the elderly by spending time listening to their stories. Or by helping them with projects they can't do for themselves anymore.

You can assist and bring moments of blessing to older people. They can make you glad you did.

Reflection: Do you know any elderly people who seem to be ignored? How can you show them some extra kindness and respect for their age?

Prayer Point: *Lord, thank you for the wisdom you have given older people. Help me remember that I can learn a lot from them, and help me be kind and respectful to them.*

The Most Helpless People of All

"'Before I formed you in the womb I knew you, before you were born I set you apart...'" –Jeremiah 1:5

Have you ever read books by Dr. Seuss? If so, you might remember the line from *Horton Hears a Who*, "A person's a person no matter how small!" That's how God feels about children, even before they are born. He's the one who gives them life and knits them together.

Sometimes women get pregnant when they weren't planning on it. Those babies aren't a mistake or an accident in God's eyes. They are still his beloved image-bearers. But we can measure the value of human beings in the wrong way.

Did you know, in many parts of the world, including America, it is legal to kill a baby before it's born? Some people think if a human being is too tiny and helpless to talk, he or she is not really a person yet. So it's okay to end their life.

Sometimes a woman is really poor, or she already has lots of kids, or she's ashamed she got pregnant, so she's scared about having the baby. Because of the world's wrong way of thinking about human beings and their value, she could decide to have an abortion. A doctor would remove the baby from her belly before it's big enough to survive on its own.

I know that forcing a baby to die sounds really terrible. And it is. God feels angry and sad when this happens. Mothers who have had abortions, and fathers who are a part of that decision, often feel lots of guilt and sadness later. Their hearts are broken, because they didn't understand the idea about God's image-bearers until too late.

Our country's law allows babies to be killed before birth, but God's law does not (Jeremiah 7:31)! We must do what we can to protect God's tiniest image-bearers.

Jesus always reached out to the people whom others considered the least important. He knows every image-bearer, even before they're formed in their mother's belly. He cares about each one.

Reflection: In light of how much God values every one of his image-bearers, try to imagine how he feels when his most helpless, innocent children are destroyed before they are born. How do you feel when you think about this?

Prayer Point: *Lord, thank you that every image-bearer is marvelously made from the very beginning of their lives. Please help people think correctly about preborn babies and be willing to protect them.*

Amazing Grace

"Therefore, there is now no condemnation for those who are in Christ Jesus, because through Christ Jesus the law of the Spirit who gives life has set you free from the law of sin and death." – Romans 8:1-2

How hard to know babies can die by abortion. Since God has given us a sense of justice, we may feel angry at people who make this decision. We may feel they deserve to go to jail or be punished in some other way.

Are mothers and fathers who have done this to their children worse than other sinners? On the one hand, God sees all sin as the same. Whether the sin is lying or cheating or pride, it separates us from God (James 2:10). On the other hand, some kinds of sins have more severe consequences (John 19:11). Destroying a helpless, innocent human is a very serious thing.

Thankfully, through his death and resurrection, Jesus paid for every kind of sin. When mothers and fathers who have chosen abortion come to him and confess the wrong they've done, he forgives them. But their hearts must be healed, and the sadness may never go away completely.

Jesus shows mercy to sinners, including people who caused their babies to die. So we must show mercy in our attitude toward them, too. Most people don't want to have an abortion. They do it because they feel they don't have a choice. That doesn't make it okay, but it helps us be understanding.

A pregnancy center is a place where women can go when they find out they might be pregnant and they are upset about it. I worked at a pregnancy center for a long time. We helped those who already had an abortion and felt bad and sad. We showed them what the Bible says about God's forgiveness. We prayed with them. We helped them have a special ceremony so they could remember God values the tiny image-bearers they lost.

We watched women and men change from being depressed and hopeless to being joyful because of God's forgiveness. It's like God glued together the pieces of a cracked mirror to reflect him again.

God heals hearts from all kinds of sin, including abortion.

Reflection: Have you ever seen the difference between someone feeling terribly guilty about something, and then feeling wonderfully happy that God has forgiven them? Have you ever felt that way?

Prayer Point: *Lord, thank you for your mercy and forgiveness, and that you forgive every kind of sin—we just have to ask. Help me understand how serious sin can be, but also to be forgiving toward people the same way you are.*

Section Reflection: Pushed-Aside People

In this section we've seen many examples of people who might be ignored, bullied, or even killed. Now you have a better idea of the importance of understanding every human being is created by God to reflect his image.

God made us all, whether we're born with arms and legs or not. He made some of us really good at certain things, while others might have a hard time keeping up with the class. He created people who have fancy homes, and those whose belongings fit in a paper sack.

He made people of every race and skin color. He made the people who know Jesus, and those who don't know him yet. He created boys and girls happy about how they were created, as well as those who feel disappointed or confused.

Sick or injured humans are still his wonderful image-bearers. When they grow older and can't do as much anymore, he still values them. The moment a tiny baby starts growing in a mother's belly, God already values him or her as much as an adult.

When you have a friendship with Jesus, he will help you feel the way he does about people. You may get angry about wrong things done against them.

Your feelings can reflect God's feelings, and lead you into taking action steps. In the next section, we'll look at some ways you can fight evil in the world, and show brave love.

Part 4

Fighting Evil with Good

"Do not be overcome by evil, but overcome evil with good." –Romans 12:21

Be an Example

"Don't let anyone look down on you because you are young, but set an example for the believers in speech, in conduct, in love, in faith and in purity."
–1Timothy 4:12

Wow, we've covered a lot of ground in this book! You've learned some super important things to help you release your brave love on a world that needs you.

God created everything. But out of all his creation, human beings rate as most special to him. The ancient Romans thought only their emperor bore the image of God. However, Christians understand every human being bears God's image. Each one reflects his nature better than his other creatures. We were created to take care of the earth.

Because we are so special to God, we have an enemy called Satan who tries to trick us into disobeying God (I Peter 5:8). But we also have a rescuer, Jesus, who saves us from being stuck in cycles of sin. When we see people the way Jesus sees them, we recognize the amazing beauty and glory he put into them.

God wants us be kind to different kinds of people – including ourselves! He especially wants us to show brave love by reaching out to the ignored or put down or left out. He wants us to bring his kingdom to the earth by living like Jesus.

God will create a new earth one day (Revelation 21:1-5). Until then, Christians will keep bringing good changes to our world, one friendship at a time. Together we'll take action steps to fight evil.

Are you too young to make a difference? No! Kids can do great things for God. Jesus said, "Let the little children come to me, and do not hinder them, for the kingdom of God belongs to such as these (Luke 18:16)." The kingdom of God is all about showing his image-bearers worth and value. You can totally do that.

Are you getting excited thinking about how you might be able to show brave love to others? I'm excited, too! We'll go over some ways you can fight evil. I think you'll really like these ideas for how to mend our broken world. You might come up with even more ideas yourself.

Reflection: You can be an example, not only to other kids, but also to adults. How might your attitude and actions help an adult treat others better?

Prayer Point: *Lord Jesus, thank you that I don't have to wait until I'm grown up to do things for you and with you. Help me set a good example to others as I learn to show all people value.*

Day 32

Eyes like Jesus

"Do not be overcome by evil, but overcome evil with good." –Romans 12:21

There's plenty of evil in the world. The way Christians fight evil is by doing good. We look for ways to protect people being treated badly. But before you jump in to help, there's something very important you need to do. You need to ask for eyes to see individuals the way Jesus sees them.

Jesus sees two things which most of us overlook. First, he sees beauty in every single person. We look on the surface and judge by what everyone thinks at first glance. But there is so much more to human beauty than certain kinds of faces and bodies (1 Samuel 16:7).

Every human being reflects God's glory.

Second, Jesus sees people others don't notice. He looks for the put down, picked on, and pushed aside. When Jesus walked the earth, he sought those no one else noticed.

Jesus took time to bless children. His disciples thought he should be busy with adults. Jesus talked to women. In Bible times, they held less importance than men. Jesus talked to sinners and to non-Jews. Jewish leaders criticized him for that.

Jesus didn't care what critics said. He knew who he needed to serve. He wanted us to understand how we should treat each other. After Jesus died, was buried, and rose from the dead, he returned to heaven. But he promised his Holy Spirit would live inside his followers (Acts 1:8).

Now, we have the power to be like Jesus to other people! He helps us recognize they each express his glory. He helps us care about the ignored and forgotten.

He empowers us to win over evil by doing good deeds.

Reflection: Fighting evil doesn't have to be a big show. Spend a few minutes thinking about the best way you can fight evil with quiet, obedient, humble good deeds.

Prayer Point: *Lord, help me to notice the people others ignore and overlook, and help me see their beauty in your eyes. Help me to fight evil by doing good as you lead me in a way that is wise and safe.*

Do it Afraid

"'. . . Be strong and courageous. Do not be afraid; do not be discouraged, for the Lord your God will be with you wherever you go.'" –Joshua 1:9

It is good and right to show love to other people, and not play favorites with certain groups. But loving others is often hard.

It's difficult to reach out to the people who have been pushed aside by others. Often, they've been pushed aside because people feel nervous around them. They don't know how to act when they talk to them.

I once knew a young girl with a disease which made her face look badly burned. This girl had her own glory and beauty, just like every image-bearer, but I had to get used to looking at her very different face.

Hanging out with people in wheelchairs, or who can't talk right, or who can't see or hear can be a challenge. Sometimes it's hard to figure out a person's struggle, so we're not sure what they need from us. We can get nervous about making a mistake, so we stay away instead.

For instance, talking to a homeless person who lives outdoors and has such big needs can be scary. Or understanding people from other countries or other religions or races seems hard at first.

Real love requires being brave, and perhaps, to be willing

to do hard work (Mark 12:30-31). We must attempt to understand people different than us. We also must be careful and wise, because sometimes it can be difficult to tell which people really need and want our help. Adults like your parents can help you figure this out.

It's okay to feel scared when you come across a pushed-aside person. Having brave love doesn't mean you don't feel nervous. Brave love chooses to reach out anyway—even if you're afraid.

Reflection: Think of someone you've met who is in a wheelchair, or whose face or body looks really different in some way—someone you didn't know how to approach. How can you train yourself to be kindly confident toward them?

Prayer Point: *Lord, thank you that I don't have to wait until I feel brave to do good deeds. Help me to reach out to people even when I feel scared, because you are with me and will help me.*

Does Love Mean You Have to Agree?

"Instead, speaking the truth in love, we will grow to become in every respect the mature body of him who is the head, that is, Christ." –*Ephesians 4:15*

Some people think Christians aren't very loving. Maybe they've met Christians who presented a poor example of Jesus. Or they don't want to follow God's rules, so they point fingers at Christians as an excuse. Or they presume loving someone means you have to agree with any opinion or action they make.

For example, some people today believe if a boy and girl is confused about how God made them, the kindest thing we can do is to accept their mixed-up feelings as the truth. They even think we should help them have surgery if they feel they were born with the wrong body. If we don't agree with their decision, we are being mean.

God created everyone, and he is wise and good. God says it's wrong and against his natural order for men to marry men, or for women to marry women, or to change from male to female or female to male (Romans 1:18-25).

God created us as male and female on purpose. He knows what is best for us. Our bodies are a very important part of us. We dishonor our bodies *and* God if we don't obey his commands about them. In fact, our bodies are so important that the Holy Spirit lives inside us once we decide to follow

Jesus. They are a living temple for him (1 Corinthians 6:18-20). They belong to God.

You don't have to agree with someone in order to love them. Agreeing with people when they go against God's commands is a way to be nice, but not kind. Sharing God's truth is the best starting point for real love between friends.

If you know someone who is confused about being a boy or girl, you can tell them God didn't make a mistake. You can explain his rules to them, and show them God's love.

Here's how: stick up for them when others put them down. Reach out to them when they're lonely. Ask good questions to find out their needs and wants. What makes them sad, mad, or happy? What makes them laugh?

Real love isn't a feeling. It's an action that sticks with God's truth.

Reflection: Have you heard people say things like "Christians are haters" because we disagree with others? Do you think disagreeing with someone's behavior is the same as hating them? Why or why not?

____

____

____

____

____

____

____

____

____

____

____

____

Prayer Point: *Lord, thank you that I don't have to choose between speaking the truth and loving people, because you tell me to do both. Please help me show love toward people with whom I disagree, and help me be kind and truthful even if people call me names for doing it.*

You can Help in Your Town

"Whatever your hand finds to do, do it with all your might..." –Ecclesiastes 9:10

When a woman is scared or upset about being pregnant, she can visit a pregnancy center. The Christians who work there give moms and dads support and help. They don't need to end their baby's life.

Pregnancy centers save lives!

Each year, many centers sponsor a special event called a "Walk for Life." People of all ages ask others to sponsor them for the walk and sign up for whatever amount they want to give. Afterward, the center receives the money donated so they can continue saving babies' lives.

For several years, a young girl brought the most money into our center during the Walk for Life. Starting as a nine-year-old, this girl boldly asked lots of people to back her. Each year, she collected about a thousand dollars.

You can help save lives by participating in a Walk for Life, too!

A pregnancy center protects unborn children, those who cannot speak for themselves. So getting sponsors for a Walk for Life is one great idea for how a kid can win over evil by doing good.

You can also look into other possibilities for showing value to pushed-aside people, like serving meals for homeless folks at a soup kitchen. Or visiting lonely elderly people at a nursing home (I John 3:17-18). Your parents may have some ideas, and your church might be able to help, too.

In fact, so many kinds of people need help you could find it hard to decide what to do.

Ask God where he wants you to put your time and energy. He will give you wisdom and help. Ask your mom and dad for guidance, too. Focus on what you need to do right now, in a way that is wise and safe.

Reflection: Think about some of the ways your church helps people in your town—elderly people, homeless people, unborn children who need protection, and others. What adults can assist you with this? What kinds of people do you feel excited about helping?

Prayer Point: *Lord, thank you for the many chances I have to help others. Since there are so many needs, please give me wisdom about where you want me to give some time and energy.*

You can Help around the Globe

"Here is my servant whom I have chosen, the one I love, in whom I delight; I will put my Spirit on him, and he will proclaim justice to the nations." –Matthew 12:18

Most people in America enjoy a pretty comfortable life. We can turn on a faucet and get hot or cold running water any time we want. We can refrigerate our food, and turn on the heater when we're cold. We own cars to get around.

It's not so easy in other parts of the world. One time, we ate dinner with friends from Uganda. They said, "Oh, I like your water! We have to walk a long way for ours."

Poor people there face danger. Young girls in Africa often have to walk long distances by themselves to fetch water for their family. If a man jumps out of the bushes and grabs a girl, no one stops him from doing terrible things to her. Sometimes adults kidnap children to sell as slaves to people far away, where no one can find them.

Girls face even greater risk than boys. That's because, in many parts of the world, boys hold more value than girls—even before they are born. Millions of preborn baby girls have been killed because they are not boys.

In some countries, girls don't get to go to school. They learn only how to take care of a home. They don't exercise the amazing mind God gave them. Or learn a business. They can't earn money for themselves. They have no power and no way to protect themselves from harsh treatment. In some places, things haven't changed since Bible times!

In at least two ways, you can help protect pushed-aside people in other parts of the world right now (Micah 6:8). First, you can pray. This is the best way to battle against evil. Then God can show you what to do next.

Second, you can collect money for one of the organizations listed in the back of this book.

Remember the boy who gave Jesus his loaves and fishes? Jesus fed 5,000 people with his offerings (John 6:1-15). Don't worry about what amount you give. Jesus can multiply it beyond your imagination.

Reflection: In the back of this book, I've listed Christian organizations that help God's image-bearers in other countries. Some especially protect girls from being treated unjustly or even killed. Others help whole villages get clean water. Think about how you would most like to help.

Prayer Point: *Lord, thank you that I have such a comfortable life in my country. Help me to remember those who do not, and show me how I can help fight evil around the world with my prayers and my generosity.*

Good News and Hard Times

"'Blessed are you when people insult you, persecute you and falsely say all kinds of evil against you because of me. Rejoice and be glad, because great is your reward in heaven…'" – Matthew 5:11-12

We can do a lot of good things for people in other nations. Like provide clean water. Or send medicine and doctors to heal sick people. Or supply seeds to help families avoid hunger by learning to grow food.

Christians do these good deeds because we care about the whole person—body, mind and soul. However, not knowing Jesus presents a bigger problem than having a hungry stomach. So we do what we can to help provide practical needs. But we also want people to know about Jesus and what he has done for them. Then they will experience eternal life—not just a few meals.

Something else happens in other countries.

In some foreign places, the most put-down, picked-on, and pushed-aside people are Christians! This is called *persecution*. Christians can lose their jobs, be taken away from their families, and even be beaten or killed for believing in Jesus. Sometimes church buildings get shut down or destroyed.

This happened in Bible times, too. Jesus warned such things would happen to some of us (Matt. 24:9-13). He also promised great rewards to Christians who suffer in these ways.

Christians are God's image-bearers with a double measure of *doxa*—we reflect God's glory. The Holy Spirit lives inside us to shine his glory, too. Many glorious image-bearers who live in other lands need protection. They are our brothers and sisters in Christ, so we must care and show concern for them.

You can help these Christians by praying for God's safekeeping and comfort in hard times. Pray for them to have strong faith. Pray they are able to forgive their enemies, and that their enemies will become Christians, too. That wonderful miracle happens sometimes.

Be very thankful you live in a country with clean water and good food, and where we can still worship God freely. Let's also remember the Christians who face hardships in other countries.

Reflection: Imagine what it would be like to go to jail or be beaten for singing worship songs in your own house, or reading your Bible, or talking to a neighbor about Jesus. That would be really tough to take. In the back of the book, I've listed some organizations that tell you how to pray for Christians who suffer this way.

____

____

____

____

____

____

____

____

____

____

____

Prayer Point: *Lord, thank you that I live in a country where I can worship you without getting in trouble. Help me to remember Christians in other countries and to pray for them.*

Who Gets to be Jesus?

"The King will reply, 'Truly I tell you, whatever you did for one of the least of these brothers and sisters of mine, you did for me.'" –Matthew 25:40

When Christians do good deeds, we become the hands and feet of Jesus. We represent Christ to the world. His followers keep on bringing his kingdom to the earth by living in a way that pleases him.

Representing Jesus is a great privilege. We can feel good about that. But there's another side to this truth. According to the Bible, it's actually the people we help who become like Jesus to us!

Jesus said if we feed hungry people, or give clothes to those who don't have any, or visit people stuck in prison, or show hospitality to people we don't know very well, we do these things for him (Matt. 25:31-46).

What a great honor to do good things for pushed-aside image-bearers.

One time, I heard a man tell the story of his daughter, who died as a teenager. All her life, this girl endured lots of problems. She couldn't care for herself. She didn't talk. She was unable to do things for other people.

But she never complained. She allowed her dad take care of her, which he did with a good attitude. This dad understood his daughter represented Jesus. Taking care of her gave him a chance to serve Christ.

Perhaps we feel proud of ourselves for doing good things for other people. We might think we're pretty awesome because we treat God's image-bearers better than others do.

However, it's our privilege to serve pushed-aside people. Jesus feels we're doing these good things to him. So instead of pushed-aside people thanking us for our kindness, maybe we should thank them.

They allow us to serve Jesus.

Reflection: The next time you help in a soup kitchen, or visit an elderly person, or show kindness to someone disabled, think about this: you are doing it for Jesus. He is well pleased with you!

____

____

____

____

____

____

____

____

____

____

____

____

Prayer Point: *Lord Jesus, Thank you for the chances other people give me to do things for you. Help me always remember that I am doing good deeds, not just for that person, but for you.*

Heavenly Rewards

"His master replied, 'Well done, good and faithful servant! You have been faithful with a few things; I will put you in charge of many things. Come and share your master's happiness!'" –Matthew 25:23

When my kids were younger, our church took on a building project. The work included adding walls, installing carpet, and painting. My oldest son, 13-year-old Danny, promised the men at church he'd help one afternoon.

However, Danny needed a ride to the church, and I didn't feel good the day he signed up to help. So I couldn't drive him. Danny got mad and left the house to cool off.

Later, I went out to our garage. The whole place was straightened up and cleaned out! Since Danny couldn't help at church, he worked at home instead.

Danny pleased me the way he vented his frustrated feelings by being useful. Right away, his father and I bought him a whole box of football cards to reward his good choice.

When our three sons were all teenagers, it was our family's turn to clean our church's building. Usually, all five of us did this big job together. This time, my husband and I couldn't make it, so our boys cleaned the whole church by themselves.

They did a great job. As soon as we had some time off, we rewarded them by taking them on a special trip.

God loves to reward his children, too (Hebrews 11:6). He knows our hearts. We get tired and discouraged in doing what's right. We need a "Good job!" from him.

Jesus notices every little act we do for others, even if no one else notices. He will reward your obedience in a much bigger way than football cards, trips to fun places, or new clothes. He will give you rewards that last forever!

Reflection: Have you ever thought about what our heavenly rewards might look like? Consider how much Jesus loves you, and that he is the Lord of all. What he gives us is going to be pretty great—and the best part of all is we get to enjoy him forever!

Prayer Point: *Lord, thank you for being a good Father, and for rewarding your children. I'm grateful that you promise me a reward, and most of all I'm excited that one day I will get to see you face to face!*

Pilgrims on a Broken Planet

"...they were longing for a better country—a heavenly one. Therefore God is not ashamed to be called their God, for he has prepared a city for them." –Hebrews 11:16

In 1620, colonists from England settled in this country so they could worship God the way they wanted to. We call them Pilgrims. A pilgrim is one who journeys in foreign lands, or one who travels to a holy place to worship God.

Did you know that, as a follower of Jesus, you are a pilgrim, too?

Following Jesus means knowing this life measures very short compared to forever. We learn to care more about eternity than about right now. When we don't feel as comfortable and happy as we'd like to, we're willing to wait for better things. Our reward will be great in heaven.

The heavens and the earth will be renewed one day. Everyone who says "yes" to Jesus will be completely happy when that day comes (Isaiah 65:17-25). Like brand-new mirrors with no more cracks, we will reflect God's image the way he created us to do.

Meanwhile, we love and worship Jesus, our rescuer.

We act as his hands and feet in a broken world, among the put down, picked on, and pushed aside. We feel the same as Jesus about injustice. We protect others when we're able. We value those nobody else does. We help in whatever way we can.

In honor we treat those Jesus calls “the least of these” with respect and kindness. We do these good things for him. We tell others the good news about him. And he promises to be with us through the Holy Spirit until he returns. (Matthew 28:18-20).

You are a pilgrim traveling with other pilgrims. You’re on a trip. You can show your love for Jesus by treasuring every single image-bearer near you.

Reflection: Have you ever been on a really long trip? Did it almost feel kind of weird to come back to your house? We are pretty used to this world the way it is, but God will make it all brand-new one day. In the meantime, he shows us how to show brave love here and now.

Prayer Point: *Lord, thank you that this world in its present shape is not our real home. Thank you for preparing a heavenly home for us. Thank you for helping me to show your wonderful love to other people. I love you so much!*

Section Reflection: Fighting Evil with Good

So now you know a kid can fight evil in very important ways. You see, in God's kingdom, things are upside down from the way we are used to thinking. In God's kingdom, small is big, weak is powerful, and a little bit is a lot.

You can have a big influence in this world by the way you treat your fellow humans. You can be an example, even to adults. Look for the beauty in all people. Notice the ones everyone ignores. Reach out with brave love in wise and safe ways, even when you're nervous or scared. You can be a real friend to people you disagree with, too. Your parents and other adults at church can advise you with this.

You can pray and raise money and take action right in your own town. You can also bring aid to needy people in other countries around the world. When you give, you serve Jesus. He will reward you with a forever kind of reward.

You are a pilgrim on this earth who knows the real, true story about the world and God and humanity. You know we're especially created to reflect God's image the way a mirror or photo does. That image has been cracked and broken, and we can't fix ourselves. But one day, everyone who trusts in Jesus as their rescuer will enjoy life forever in a restored world. We won't be broken anymore.

Until then, God will give you brave love. When you release yours, others will know how much they matter to him. Finding ways to show people God's love produces the greatest adventure of your life!

Afterword

Congratulations! You've completed a forty-lesson adventure of exploring how God feels about human beings. You have a more solid understanding of how much he values us and why.

People are different from animals, because we were created just a little bit lower than the angels. By knowing people, we get a peek at what God is like. Humans reflect his nature in a special way. Even though we're broken, we shine with a special honor and splendor called glory. Christians have a double dose of this glory, because the Holy Spirit lives inside them.

Now it's time to release your brave love and reach out to some pushed-aside people! Maybe you already have some ideas on what you'd like to do. What special person or group of people has God put on your heart? I encourage you to talk with your parents about your ideas. They can give you wise guidelines in taking doable action steps.

Your mom and dad might want to read some of the books I've listed for them. You could talk about those books together as a family. You'll learn even more about things like how Christians have changed the world for the better, why it makes so much sense to believe what the Bible says, and how we can trust what God says even when most people don't obey his rules.

In the Bible, the number forty stands for transformation—change, renewal, do over. I'm praying God will fill you with a brave love that comes from him. I'm also praying you'll always know how much you mean to him and that you'll see people around you the way he does.

May your brave love be released to overcome evil with good, all of your life!

God bless you,

Susanne

Acknowledgements

A book may have one author, but there's always a whole team behind the scenes.

I'm grateful to my husband Scott and to Daniel and Amanda, Samuel and Jameson, and Jedidiah and Rebecca. Our family life inspired this book. I have bounced every detail off you guys, and your feedback has been very helpful.

Amanda, thanks for your inspired suggestion of the theme of *Imago Dei*. Sam, thanks for your time and effort double-checking the manuscript for theological accuracy and appropriate Scripture references. Thanks to Jamé for your eyes, as well. All of you have been so supportive, and for this I am grateful.

Janet Bly, thank you so much for all of your wisdom and encouragement—and for editing this manuscript! You have the heart of a teacher, and you've been a God-send in many ways.

Thank you to my prayer partners, Marilyn Steingruber, Wendy Neal, and Pam Thorson. Pam, I'm so grateful for a writing friend with whom I can ride the ridges.

Thank you as well to those who uphold Scott and me on a regular basis—pastors Kevin Beeson, Moses Latella, and Hugh Laybourn, as well as Shelleigh Beeson, Cindy Latella, Lyndal

Stoutin, Sherry Stoutin, Clare McCracken and Ange Movius. This book would not exist without the prayer that happened behind the scenes.

Special thanks for pre-reading this manuscript, from the time it was half-finished, to Ange Movius, along with daughter Rosalyn. Your input helped shape this book into what it was destined to be.

Thanks to Bernice Seward, children's author, for your detailed input on the manuscript. Your eyes were helpful! Thanks to Stephanie Herbert for additional suggestions.

Thank you to my publisher, the team at Create Space/ Kindle Direct Publishing, and all of your support and help. Thanks, Ken Raney, for the bright and inviting cover which beautifully captures the heart of this book. Thanks to Nick Caya and the team at Word-to-Kindle for the lovely job on the interior design.

I'm especially grateful to my parents for raising me with the understanding that loving and serving Jesus matters most. I miss you, Papa, and I'm glad I'll see you again one day. Thank you, Mama, for your love and prayers.

Most of all, I offer thanks and praise to the Lord Jesus for allowing me the privilege of inspiring young readers to release the brave love he has given them. May he receive glory and honor through this book.

Further Reading and Resources for Parents:

Apologetics & the Gospel:

Talking with your Kids about God, Natasha Crain

Thestorymaker.com (short video on the gospel)

Total Truth, Nancy Pearcey

Why I Believe, Chip Ingram

Church and Culture:

Axis.org (weekly "culture translator," video interviews, parent guides, etc.)

Breakpoint.org with Eric Metaxas and John Stonestreet (radio show and blog)

How Christianity Changed the World, Alvin Schmidt

Global Ministries:

Compassion.com (sponsor a child in poverty)

Ijm.org (International Justice Mission fights slavery and provides aftercare)

Persecution.com (news and prayer requests from "Voice of the Martyrs")

Worldvision.org (sponsor a child in poverty)

Worldwatchmonitor.org (news and prayer requests about persecuted Christians)

Healthy Self-image for Kids:

Celebratekids.com (Dr. Kathy Koch offers several books and other resources)

Healthy Sexuality:

A Parent's Guide to Preventing Homosexuality, Joseph Nicolosi

A Practical Guide to Culture, John Stonestreet and Brett Kunkle

Love Thy Body, Nancy Pearcey

About the Author

Susanne Maynes is a certified Biblical Counselor with the Board of Christian Professional and Pastoral Counselors and holds a Bachelor of Arts degree in Social Science from Bethany University. After home schooling her children, Susanne ministered at a pregnancy help center for ten years. This inspired her to write her first book, ***Unleashing Your Courageous Compassion***: *40 Reflections on Rescuing the Unborn.*

Susanne blogs on topics of church and culture, spiritual growth and Christian parenting at ***susannemaynes.com***. As part of her "Passionate Parenting" ministry, she teaches an online course and weekend workshop called "How to Raise Wholehearted Followers of Jesus" (see ***passionateparenting.thinkific.com***). She blogs regularly for Heartbeat International, a pro-life organization, at ***pregnancyhelpnews.com***, and speaks in a variety of settings.

Susanne and her husband, Scott, have been married for 35 years and live in Idaho. They have three grown sons, three daughters-in-law, and four grandchildren (with more on the way). Susanne enjoys the great outdoors, having tea with friends, and reading to her grandkids.

To contact Susanne:

susannemaynes.com

passionateparenting.thinkific.com (online course)

facebook.com/AuthorSusanneMaynes

twitter.com/susannemaynes

If you enjoyed this book, please tell others about it and consider writing a review at your favorite online bookstore, such as Amazon, or on social media, such as Goodreads.

Made in the USA
San Bernardino, CA
02 December 2018